TABLE OF CONTENTS

MARKETING AUTOMATION: INVESTIGATE HOW AI STREAMLINES MARKETING TASKS, AUTOMATES WORKFLOW, AND IMPROVES CAMPAIGN MANAGEMENT

BY
HENRY E. PARKINS

COPYRIGHT PAGE

ECO-FRIENDLY CRAFTING WITH AI: A GUIDE TO CREATING CRAFTS USING SUSTAINABLE AND UPCYCLED MATERIALS, PROMOTING ENVIRONMENTAL CONSCIOUSNESS IN CRAFTING PROJECTS USING AI

73

MARKETING AUTOMATION: INVESTIGATE HOW AI STREAMLINES MARKETING TASKS, AUTOMATES WORKFLOW, AND IMPROVES CAMPAIGN MANAGEMENT

73

INTRODUCTION

In the dynamic landscape of the digital age, businesses are constantly seeking innovative strategies to stay ahead in the highly competitive market. Marketing, as a pivotal component of any successful enterprise, has witnessed a transformative revolution propelled by technology. At the forefront of this evolution stands marketing automation, a paradigm shift that has redefined how businesses engage with their audience, nurture leads, and optimize their campaigns.

Brief Overview of the Significance of Marketing Automation in the Digital Age

Marketing automation, a multifaceted approach that utilizes technology to streamline and automate marketing processes, has emerged as a cornerstone in the arsenal of modern businesses. The digital era has ushered in a deluge of data, channels, and customer touchpoints, necessitating a sophisticated and efficient method to navigate this complex landscape. Marketing automation addresses this challenge by providing a comprehensive solution that not only enhances efficiency but also allows marketers to craft personalized and targeted campaigns at scale.

In an environment where consumer behaviors are constantly evolving, the ability to adapt swiftly is paramount. Marketing automation empowers organizations to respond dynamically to these changes, enabling them to deliver the right message to the right audience at the right time. As we embark on this exploration into the realm of marketing automation, we will delve into its profound impact on reshaping marketing strategies, amplifying customer engagement, and ultimately driving business success in the digital age.

Introduction to AI and Its Role in Streamlining Marketing Tasks

At the heart of the marketing automation revolution lies the transformative power of Artificial Intelligence (AI). AI, with its ability to analyze vast datasets, discern patterns, and make data-driven predictions, has become the linchpin in streamlining marketing tasks. By harnessing the capabilities of AI, marketers can transcend traditional boundaries, moving beyond manual processes and tapping into a realm of unprecedented efficiency and precision.

In this exploration, we will unravel the various facets of AI that contribute to the enhancement of marketing automation. From intelligent customer segmentation to the automation of intricate workflow processes, AI plays a pivotal role in optimizing every stage of the marketing journey. As we investigate the symbiotic relationship between AI and marketing automation, we will uncover how these technologies converge to not only alleviate the burden of routine tasks but also

13

empower marketers to unlock new dimensions of creativity and strategic thinking.

CHAPTER 1

THE EVOLUTION OF MARKETING AUTOMATION

Historical Perspective on Marketing Automation

In the annals of marketing, the quest for efficiency and precision has been an enduring pursuit. The roots of marketing automation can be traced back to the early 20th century when businesses sought ways to systematize and optimize their promotional efforts. However, it wasn't until the advent of computers and the proliferation of digital technologies that the true potential of marketing automation began to unfold.

The early days of marketing automation were marked by rudimentary attempts to streamline manual processes. Simple tools and techniques, such as mail merge functionalities and basic customer databases, laid the foundation for the more sophisticated automation we see today. These modest beginnings, while groundbreaking at the time, foreshadowed the transformative journey that marketing automation would embark upon in the digital age.

Key Milestones in the Development of Marketing Automation Tools

1960s-1970s: Emergence of Database Marketing

The precursor to modern marketing automation, this era saw the utilization of early databases for storing customer information. Companies began to experiment with segmenting their audience based on various criteria.

1980s: Rise of Direct Marketing Software

With the introduction of personal computers, businesses started leveraging software solutions to manage direct marketing campaigns. This period witnessed the initial integration of technology to automate certain aspects of marketing tasks.

1990s: Web-Based Marketing Automation

The rise of the internet brought about a paradigm shift in marketing. Web-based automation tools emerged, enabling marketers to track website interactions and gather valuable data on user behavior.

2000s: Integration of Customer Relationship Management (CRM)

The integration of CRM systems marked a pivotal moment, allowing businesses to synchronize customer data across departments. This laid the groundwork for more comprehensive marketing automation platforms.

17

2010s: The Era of Advanced Automation Solutions

The last decade witnessed a surge in the sophistication of marketing automation tools. Machine learning algorithms, predictive analytics, and multi-channel automation became integral components, providing marketers with unprecedented insights and capabilities.

The Role of AI in Shaping the Future of Marketing Automation

As we traverse through the historical evolution of marketing automation, it becomes evident that Artificial Intelligence (AI) is the linchpin propelling this evolution into the future. The integration of AI introduces a level of intelligence and adaptability that goes beyond the capabilities of traditional automation.

AI is poised to redefine marketing automation by bringing about a seismic shift in how businesses interact with their audience. From predictive analytics that forecast customer behavior to machine learning algorithms that enhance personalization, AI is at the forefront of shaping a new era for marketing automation. In the subsequent chapters, we will delve deeper into the various facets of AI, exploring how it augments marketing tasks, automates workflows, and fundamentally improves the management of campaigns in the contemporary digital landscape. The evolution of marketing automation is an enthralling journey, and AI stands as the beacon guiding its trajectory into the future.

CHAPTER 2

UNDERSTANDING AI IN MARKETING

Definition and Explanation of Artificial Intelligence in the Marketing Context

In the realm of marketing, Artificial Intelligence (AI) represents a paradigm shift, offering a spectrum of advanced technologies designed to emulate human intelligence. At its core, AI in marketing involves the development of systems that can analyze vast datasets, derive meaningful insights, and make informed decisions without explicit human programming.

In the marketing context, AI acts as a catalyst for transforming data into actionable strategies. It encompasses various subfields, including machine learning, natural language processing, and computer vision, each contributing unique capabilities to enhance marketing processes. AI enables marketers to move beyond traditional rule-based automation, facilitating adaptive and intelligent decision-making.

Types of AI Used in Marketing Automation: Machine Learning (ML)

ML algorithms enable systems to learn patterns and make predictions based on data. In marketing, ML is employed for predictive analytics, customer segmentation, and recommendation engines. It allows for dynamic adjustments to marketing strategies based on evolving trends and consumer behaviors.

Natural Language Processing (NLP):

NLP empowers machines to understand, interpret, and generate human-like language. In marketing, NLP is instrumental in sentiment analysis, chatbots, and content creation. It enhances customer interactions by enabling automated systems to comprehend and respond to natural language queries.

Computer Vision:

Computer vision enables machines to interpret and make decisions based on visual data. In marketing, this technology is utilized in image recognition, video analytics, and visual content optimization. It enhances the visual aspects of marketing campaigns, providing a more personalized and engaging experience.

Predictive Analytics:

Predictive analytics leverages statistical algorithms and machine learning to forecast future trends and behaviors. In marketing, it aids in lead scoring, customer lifetime value prediction, and dynamic content optimization. Marketers can make data-driven decisions to maximize the effectiveness of their campaigns.

Benefits and Challenges of Incorporating AI into Marketing Strategies

Benefits: a. Data-Driven Decision Making:

AI processes vast datasets in real-time, enabling marketers to derive actionable insights and make informed decisions based on data.

b. Personalization at Scale:

AI facilitates hyper-personalization by analyzing customer behavior and preferences, allowing marketers to deliver targeted and relevant content to individual users.

c. Efficiency and Automation:

Automation powered by AI streamlines repetitive tasks, freeing up time for marketers to focus on strategy, creativity, and building meaningful connections with their audience.

d. Improved Customer Experience:

AI-driven technologies such as chatbots and personalized recommendations enhance the overall customer experience, fostering better engagement and loyalty.

Challenges: a. Data Quality and Privacy Concerns:

The success of AI in marketing relies on the quality and privacy of data. Ensuring data accuracy and adhering to privacy regulations are critical challenges.

b. Integration Complexity:

Integrating AI into existing marketing systems can be complex and may require significant adjustments to ensure seamless functionality.

c. Skill Gap:

The evolving nature of AI necessitates a skilled workforce. Many organizations face challenges in finding and retaining professionals with expertise in both marketing and AI.

d. Ethical Considerations:

The use of AI raises ethical concerns, such as bias in algorithms and the responsible use of customer data. Marketers must navigate these considerations to build trust with their audience.

Understanding the nuances of AI in marketing is pivotal for leveraging its benefits while addressing the associated challenges. As we proceed in this exploration, we will delve into specific applications of AI in marketing automation, unraveling the intricate ways in which it transforms marketing tasks, automates workflows, and elevates the management of campaigns in the digital landscape.

CHAPTER 3

CORE COMPONENTS OF MARKETING AUTOMATION

Overview of the Fundamental Elements of Marketing Automation

To comprehend the intricate workings of marketing automation, it is essential to dissect its core components, each playing a pivotal role in orchestrating a seamless and effective marketing strategy. These fundamental elements form the backbone of any marketing automation system, collectively streamlining processes, enhancing engagement, and optimizing overall performance.

Customer Segmentation:

Customer segmentation involves dividing a target audience into distinct groups based on shared characteristics. This allows marketers to tailor their messages, ensuring relevance and resonance. Segmentation criteria may include demographics, behavior, and psychographics. Effective segmentation ensures that marketing efforts are personalized and targeted, enhancing the likelihood of positive responses.

Lead Scoring:

Lead scoring is the process of assigning a numerical value to leads based on their interactions with marketing touchpoints. It enables marketers to prioritize and focus efforts on leads that are more likely to convert. Factors such as engagement level, website visits, and interaction with content contribute to lead scores. This systematic approach ensures that resources are allocated efficiently, maximizing the impact of marketing campaigns.

Email Marketing:

Email marketing remains a cornerstone of marketing strategies, and automation has revolutionized its execution. Automated email campaigns can be triggered by specific actions or behaviors, delivering timely and relevant messages to the audience. From personalized welcome emails to targeted nurture sequences, automation enhances the efficiency of email marketing, fostering stronger connections with prospects and customers.

Social Media Management:

Social media has evolved into a dynamic channel for engaging with audiences. Marketing automation extends its influence to social platforms by scheduling posts, monitoring interactions, and automating responses. AI algorithms enhance social media management by analyzing user behavior, optimizing posting times, and providing insights for content creation. This integration ensures a consistent and strategic social media presence.

Analytics and Reporting:

Analytics and reporting are integral to gauging the success and impact of marketing efforts. Marketing automation platforms generate detailed reports on key performance indicators (KPIs), providing insights into campaign effectiveness, customer behavior, and ROI. AI-driven analytics go beyond traditional metrics, uncovering patterns, predicting trends, and offering actionable recommendations to refine future strategies.

How AI Enhances Each Component:

Customer Segmentation:

AI enhances customer segmentation by analyzing vast datasets to identify nuanced patterns and preferences. Machine learning algorithms can dynamically adapt segmentation criteria based on real-time data, ensuring a more accurate and responsive segmentation process.

Lead Scoring:

AI-driven lead scoring goes beyond basic criteria, incorporating predictive analytics to assess the likelihood of conversion. Machine learning models continuously learn from historical data, refining lead scoring algorithms to adapt to evolving customer behavior and market dynamics.

Email Marketing:

AI transforms email marketing by enabling hyper-personalization. Natural Language Processing (NLP) algorithms analyze customer behavior and preferences, allowing marketers to craft emails that resonate with individual recipients. AI can also optimize send times and subject lines for maximum impact.

Social Media Management:

AI in social media management analyzes user interactions, sentiment, and engagement patterns. Machine learning algorithms identify optimal posting times, suggest content topics, and automate responses to specific triggers, ensuring a strategic and adaptive social media presence.

Analytics and Reporting:

AI-powered analytics elevate reporting by providing deeper insights into data. Predictive analytics models anticipate future trends, enabling marketers to proactively adjust strategies. Natural Language Processing in reporting tools facilitates the extraction of actionable

insights from unstructured data, empowering marketers with a holistic view of campaign performance.

Understanding the symbiotic relationship between marketing automation and AI in these core components is essential for unlocking the full potential of modern marketing strategies. As we delve deeper into the exploration of marketing automation, subsequent chapters will illuminate real-world applications, case studies, and best practices, showcasing how AI streamlines marketing tasks, automates workflows, and significantly improves the management of campaigns in the contemporary digital landscape.

CHAPTER 4

WORKFLOW AUTOMATION IN MARKETING

Definition and Importance of Workflow Automation

Workflow automation stands as a cornerstone in the evolution of marketing practices, representing a systematic approach to streamline, optimize, and scale routine tasks and processes. In the context of marketing, workflow automation involves the use of technology to automate the sequential steps and actions that make up a marketing campaign or task. The primary goal is to enhance efficiency, reduce manual intervention, and ensure consistency in the execution of marketing strategies.

The importance of workflow automation in marketing cannot be overstated. As marketing campaigns grow in complexity and diversity, the need for a structured and automated approach becomes imperative. Workflow automation not only saves time but also minimizes errors, ensures adherence to timelines, and allows marketing teams to allocate resources strategically. By automating repetitive tasks, marketers can redirect their focus towards creativity, strategy, and building meaningful connections with their audience.

AI-Driven Workflow Automation Tools and Their Functionalities:

Marketing Operations Platforms:

These platforms integrate various marketing tools and channels, offering a centralized hub for managing and automating workflows. AI enhances these platforms by optimizing resource allocation, predicting campaign outcomes, and suggesting improvements based on historical data.

Campaign Orchestration Tools:

AI-driven campaign orchestration tools automate the coordination of diverse marketing channels and touchpoints. They ensure a seamless and synchronized customer experience across email, social media, web, and other channels. Machine learning algorithms adapt strategies in real-time, optimizing campaign performance.

Content Management Systems (CMS):

AI in CMS automates content creation, distribution, and optimization. Natural Language Processing (NLP) algorithms analyze audience preferences to suggest personalized content. AI-driven CMS platforms ensure that the right content is delivered to the right audience at the right time.

Lead Management and Nurturing Platforms:

AI enhances lead management by automating lead scoring, categorization, and nurturing. Machine learning algorithms analyze lead behavior, predicting the most effective nurturing paths. This ensures that leads progress through the sales funnel with minimal manual intervention.

Predictive Analytics Tools:

Predictive analytics, powered by AI, automates the analysis of vast datasets to forecast future trends and outcomes. These tools guide marketing decisions by providing insights into which strategies are likely to yield the best results. Marketers can adapt their workflows based on predictive analytics to stay ahead of the curve.

Real-World Examples of Successful Workflow Automation in Marketing

HubSpot Marketing Hub:

HubSpot's Marketing Hub leverages AI to automate various marketing processes, including lead scoring, email marketing, and social media posting. The platform's workflow automation features enable marketers to create, deploy, and analyze campaigns seamlessly, resulting in improved efficiency and engagement.

Adobe Marketo Engage:

Adobe Marketo Engage is a comprehensive marketing automation platform that utilizes AI to enhance workflow automation. The platform automates lead scoring, nurtures leads through personalized journeys, and optimizes marketing campaigns based on predictive analytics. This results in more effective and targeted marketing efforts.

Salesforce Pardot:

Salesforce Pardot integrates AI to automate lead generation, scoring, and nurturing. The platform's Engagement Studio allows marketers to design and automate customer journeys, ensuring a personalized and cohesive experience. AI-driven analytics provide insights for continuous improvement.

Mailchimp:

Mailchimp, a popular email marketing platform, incorporates AI to automate email campaigns. The platform uses predictive analytics to suggest optimal send times, personalize content, and automate follow-up emails based on user behavior. This automation streamlines the email marketing workflow and enhances campaign effectiveness.

Zoho MarketingHub:

Zoho MarketingHub employs AI-driven automation to streamline marketing workflows. The platform automates lead scoring, segmentation, and personalized communication. AI algorithms analyze customer interactions and provide actionable insights to refine marketing strategies and improve overall efficiency.

These real-world examples illustrate how AI-driven workflow automation tools have become integral to successful marketing operations. By adopting these technologies, businesses can not only streamline their marketing processes but also gain a competitive edge by delivering more personalized and impactful campaigns to their audience. In the subsequent chapters, we will explore additional applications of AI in campaign management and delve into the strategies for overcoming challenges associated with implementing workflow automation in marketing.

CHAPTER 5

CAMPAIGN MANAGEMENT WITH AI

The Role of AI in Optimizing Campaign Planning and Execution

The landscape of campaign management has witnessed a transformative shift with the integration of Artificial Intelligence (AI). AI plays a pivotal role in optimizing both the planning and execution phases of marketing campaigns. Its ability to analyze vast datasets, predict outcomes, and adapt strategies in real-time empowers marketers to create more effective, targeted, and responsive campaigns.

Data-Driven Insights:

AI processes extensive datasets to extract actionable insights. Marketers can leverage this data to understand customer behaviors, preferences, and trends, enabling informed decision-making in campaign planning.

Predictive Analytics:

AI's predictive analytics capabilities forecast future trends and outcomes based on historical data. This empowers marketers to anticipate shifts in the market, adapt strategies proactively, and optimize campaign planning for maximum impact.

Dynamic Campaign Optimization:

AI continuously analyzes campaign performance and adjusts strategies in real-time. This dynamic optimization ensures that campaigns remain effective and responsive to evolving customer behaviors throughout their lifecycle.

Resource Allocation:

AI assists in optimizing resource allocation by identifying the most effective channels, messages, and timing for campaigns. This ensures that marketing budgets are utilized efficiently, maximizing the return on investment (ROI) for each campaign.

Personalization and Targeting Through AI Algorithms

AI algorithms have revolutionized the concept of personalization and targeting in campaign management. By harnessing the power of machine learning, marketers can deliver highly personalized content to individual users, increasing engagement and fostering stronger connections.

Behavioral Analysis:

AI algorithms analyze user behavior across various touchpoints, allowing marketers to understand preferences and tailor content accordingly. This behavioral analysis ensures that campaigns resonate with the unique needs and interests of each recipient.

Segmentation Refinement:

AI enhances traditional segmentation by dynamically refining audience segments based on real-time data. This ensures that campaigns are targeted to the most relevant and receptive audience at any given moment.

Personalized Recommendations:

AI-driven recommendation engines analyze user interactions and preferences to provide personalized product or content recommendations. This level of personalization not only enhances the customer experience but also significantly improves conversion rates.

Adaptive Messaging:

AI algorithms adapt messaging based on user interactions, ensuring that subsequent communications align with the user's journey. This adaptability results in a more cohesive and personalized campaign experience for each individual.

Case Studies Illustrating Successful AI-Driven Campaign Management

Netflix:

Netflix utilizes AI algorithms to analyze user viewing habits and preferences. The platform then leverages this data to recommend personalized content to each subscriber, leading to increased user engagement and satisfaction.

Amazon:

Amazon employs AI for personalized product recommendations. The platform analyzes purchase history, browsing behavior, and demographic data to suggest products tailored to each user's preferences, contributing to higher conversion rates.

Spotify:

Spotify uses AI algorithms to curate personalized playlists for users based on their listening history and preferences. This level of personalization enhances the user experience and encourages continued engagement with the platform.

Starbucks:

Starbucks utilizes AI-driven personalization in its mobile app to offer customized promotions and recommendations to users. By analyzing past purchases and preferences, Starbucks creates targeted campaigns that resonate with individual customers.

Airbnb:

Airbnb leverages AI to personalize search results and recommendations for users. By analyzing user behavior and preferences, Airbnb ensures that users are presented with listings that align with their individual preferences, enhancing the overall user experience.

These case studies exemplify the tangible impact of AI-driven campaign management on user engagement, satisfaction, and business outcomes. As we navigate through the pages of this exploration, we will uncover additional strategies, best practices, and real-world applications of AI in marketing automation, solidifying its role as a transformative force in campaign management.

CHAPTER 6

OVERCOMING CHALLENGES AND ENSURING SUCCESS

Common Challenges in Implementing AI-Driven Marketing Automation

The integration of AI-driven marketing automation, while transformative, is not without its challenges. Understanding and navigating these hurdles is crucial for businesses seeking to harness the full potential of AI in their marketing strategies.

Data Quality and Integration:

Challenge: Inaccurate or incomplete data can hinder the effectiveness of AI algorithms. Integrating data from various sources poses challenges in maintaining consistency and accuracy.

Solution: Implement robust data quality processes, invest in data integration tools, and ensure data governance practices are in place.

Skill Gap and Training:

Challenge: The dynamic nature of AI requires a skilled workforce. Many organizations face challenges in finding professionals with expertise in both marketing and AI.

Solution: Invest in training programs to upskill existing teams and recruit individuals with a hybrid skill set. Collaborate with external experts or hire consultants to bridge skill gaps.

Integration Complexity:

Challenge: Integrating AI into existing marketing systems can be complex, especially for businesses with legacy infrastructure.

Solution: Prioritize platforms with seamless integration capabilities, and plan for a phased implementation approach to mitigate disruptions. Collaborate with vendors and IT teams for smooth integration.

Ethical Considerations:

Challenge: The use of AI raises ethical concerns, including bias in algorithms and responsible use of customer data.

Solution: Establish ethical guidelines for AI usage, conduct regular audits to identify and rectify biases, and ensure compliance with data protection regulations.

Cost Considerations:

Challenge: Implementing AI-driven marketing automation can be costly, particularly for smaller businesses with limited budgets.

Solution: Evaluate the return on investment (ROI) potential, prioritize essential functionalities, and explore scalable solutions. Cloud-based services and subscription models can also offer cost-effective options.

Strategies for Overcoming Obstacles and Ensuring Successful Implementation

Start with a Clear Strategy:

Define clear objectives and a roadmap for implementing AI-driven marketing automation. Align the strategy with overarching business goals to ensure a cohesive and purposeful implementation.

Invest in Education and Training:

Provide comprehensive training for marketing teams to understand the principles of AI and how it integrates with marketing strategies. Foster a culture of continuous learning to keep teams abreast of evolving technologies.

Collaborate Across Departments:

Foster collaboration between marketing, IT, and data science teams. Cross-functional collaboration ensures a holistic approach to implementation, addressing technical, data, and strategic aspects.

Prioritize Data Quality:

Implement rigorous data quality processes to ensure accuracy and completeness. Regularly audit and clean datasets, and establish data governance practices to maintain consistency.

Pilot Projects and Phased Implementation:

Start with pilot projects to test the effectiveness of AI-driven solutions in controlled environments. Gradually scale up implementation based on the success of pilot initiatives.

Best Practices for Maximizing the Benefits of Marketing Automation with AI

Continuous Monitoring and Optimization:

Regularly monitor AI algorithms and marketing automation processes. Optimize strategies based on ongoing analysis of performance metrics and customer feedback.

Customer-Centric Approach:

Keep the customer at the center of AI-driven marketing efforts. Personalize experiences based on customer preferences, and use AI to enhance customer journeys and satisfaction.

Agile and Adaptive Strategies:

Embrace agile methodologies for marketing strategies. Use AI to analyze real-time data and adapt campaigns dynamically, ensuring responsiveness to evolving market trends and customer behaviors.

Stay Informed on Regulatory Landscape:

Stay abreast of evolving data protection and privacy regulations. Ensure that AI-driven marketing practices align with legal and ethical standards, building trust with customers.

Feedback Loops and Iterative Processes:

Establish feedback loops for continuous improvement. Use insights from customer interactions and campaign performance to iteratively enhance AI algorithms and marketing strategies.

Successfully implementing AI-driven marketing automation requires a combination of strategic planning, collaborative efforts, and a commitment to ongoing refinement. As businesses navigate this transformative journey, the ability to overcome challenges and leverage best practices will be pivotal in unlocking the full potential of AI in modern marketing strategies. In the subsequent chapters, we will delve into emerging trends, future considerations, and the evolving role of marketing professionals in this dynamic landscape.

CHAPTER 7

FUTURE TRENDS IN MARKETING AUTOMATION

Emerging Technologies Shaping the Future of Marketing Automation

The landscape of marketing automation is continuously evolving, driven by advancements in technology and the quest for more efficient and personalized customer engagement. Several emerging technologies are set to reshape the future of marketing automation, offering new possibilities and enhancing the capabilities of AI-driven strategies.

5G Technology:

The widespread adoption of 5G technology is poised to revolutionize data transfer speeds and connectivity. This will enable marketers to deliver richer and more immersive content experiences in real-time, further enhancing the personalization of marketing campaigns.

Voice Search and Conversational AI:

The rise of voice search and conversational AI is changing the way consumers interact with brands. Integrating these technologies into marketing automation allows for more natural and personalized communication, fostering a deeper connection with users.

Augmented Reality (AR) and Virtual Reality (VR):

AR and VR technologies provide opportunities for immersive and interactive marketing experiences. Marketers can leverage these technologies to create engaging campaigns, allowing consumers to visualize products or services in real-world contexts.

Internet of Things (IoT):

The proliferation of IoT devices opens up new channels for collecting real-time data. Marketers can harness IoT data to gain insights into user behaviors and preferences, enabling more targeted and context-aware campaigns.

Blockchain Technology:

Blockchain offers enhanced security and transparency in data transactions. In marketing automation, blockchain can be utilized to secure customer data, verify the authenticity of ad impressions, and create trust in digital advertising ecosystems.

Predictions for the Evolution of AI in Marketing Strategies

AI-Powered Content Creation:

AI algorithms will play a more significant role in content creation, generating personalized and contextually relevant content at scale. Natural Language Processing (NLP) and machine learning will refine the art of crafting messages that resonate with diverse audiences.

Enhanced Predictive Analytics:

Predictive analytics will become more sophisticated, utilizing AI to analyze complex patterns and provide marketers with deeper insights. This will empower businesses to anticipate customer needs and behaviors with unprecedented accuracy.

AI-Driven Customer Journeys:

AI will take center stage in orchestrating end-to-end customer journeys. From the initial point of engagement to post-purchase interactions, AI algorithms will dynamically adapt strategies to deliver seamless and personalized experiences.

Autonomous Marketing Campaigns:

The future will see the rise of autonomous marketing campaigns where AI systems, with minimal human intervention, conceptualize, execute, and optimize campaigns based on real-time data and evolving market dynamics.

Exponential Growth in Chatbots and Virtual Assistants:

Chatbots and virtual assistants will become even more integral to customer interactions. AI-driven conversational agents will evolve to offer more natural and context-aware conversations, providing immediate and personalized support.

The Role of Marketing Professionals in Adapting to Future Trends

Continuous Learning and Skill Development:

Marketing professionals must commit to continuous learning to stay abreast of evolving technologies and industry trends. Upskilling in AI, data analytics, and emerging technologies will be essential to navigate the changing landscape.

Collaboration with AI:

Marketing professionals will increasingly collaborate with AI systems. Understanding how to leverage AI tools, interpret insights generated by algorithms, and integrate AI into strategic decision-making will be crucial for success.

Embracing Creativity and Strategy:

As routine tasks become automated, marketing professionals will have more time to focus on creativity and strategic thinking. The human touch in crafting compelling narratives and designing innovative campaigns will remain irreplaceable.

Data Governance and Ethical Considerations:

With the increasing reliance on data, marketing professionals will play a pivotal role in ensuring data governance and ethical considerations. Upholding privacy standards, addressing biases in algorithms, and fostering trust with consumers will be paramount.

Adaptability and Resilience:

The rapid pace of technological evolution requires marketing professionals to be adaptable and resilient. Embracing change, experimenting with new approaches, and learning from failures will be integral to staying ahead in the dynamic landscape of marketing automation.

CHAPTER 8

CONCLUSION

Recap of Key Insights and Takeaways:

Our journey through the pages of "Marketing Automation: Investigate How AI Streamlines Marketing Tasks, Automates Workflow, and Improves Campaign Management" has been a comprehensive exploration of the transformative landscape of modern marketing. Let's recap the key insights and takeaways that have unfolded in our exploration:

Evolution of Marketing Automation:

From its historical roots to the sophisticated platforms of today, marketing automation has evolved into a dynamic force reshaping how businesses engage with their audience.

Role of AI in Marketing Automation:

Artificial Intelligence (AI) has emerged as the linchpin in marketing automation, driving efficiency, personalization, and adaptability in marketing strategies.

Core Components of Marketing Automation:

We delved into the fundamental elements of marketing automation, exploring how AI enhances customer segmentation, lead scoring, email marketing, social media management, and analytics.

Workflow Automation in Marketing:

The implementation of AI-driven workflow automation was explored, unraveling how it streamlines processes, optimizes resource allocation, and enhances the overall efficiency of marketing operations.

Campaign Management with AI:

AI's role in optimizing campaign planning and execution, personalization, and targeting was elucidated through real-world examples, showcasing the tangible impact on user engagement and satisfaction.

Overcoming Challenges and Ensuring Success:

We navigated the common challenges in implementing AI-driven marketing automation, offering strategies to overcome obstacles and ensure successful integration.

Future Trends in Marketing Automation

The exploration of emerging technologies shaping the future, predictions for the evolution of AI in marketing, and the evolving role of marketing professionals set the stage for what lies ahead.

Final Thoughts on the Impact of AI in Streamlining Marketing Tasks

The impact of AI in streamlining marketing tasks is nothing short of revolutionary. From automating routine processes to providing predictive insights, AI has elevated marketing automation to new heights. The ability to analyze vast datasets, adapt strategies in real-time, and deliver personalized experiences has not only increased efficiency but has fundamentally transformed the way businesses connect with their audience.

AI's influence extends beyond efficiency gains; it has redefined the very nature of customer interactions. The power of personalization, adaptive messaging, and predictive analytics has enabled businesses to forge deeper connections with their audience, fostering loyalty and brand advocacy. The marriage of AI and marketing automation has, without a doubt, positioned businesses on the cutting edge of innovation, propelling them into a future where customer-centric strategies are paramount.

Encouragement for Marketers to Embrace the Future of Marketing Automation

As we stand on the cusp of a future shaped by emerging technologies and evolving consumer behaviors, the call for marketers is to embrace this transformative landscape. The future of marketing automation, with AI at its core, holds immense possibilities for those willing to adapt, innovate, and explore new horizons.

Embrace the ongoing journey of learning and upskilling. The fusion of creativity, strategic thinking, and AI-driven insights will propel marketing professionals into a realm where campaigns are not just automated but are intelligent, adaptive, and deeply resonant with the needs and desires of the audience.

The future belongs to those who dare to navigate uncharted territories, those who see challenges as opportunities for growth, and those who understand that the true power of marketing automation lies in its ability to humanize technology. As we conclude this exploration, let it serve as an inspiration for marketers to embark on this exciting journey with zeal, curiosity, and a commitment to shaping the future of marketing in the digital age.

CHAPTER 9

APPENDIX

Glossary of Key Terms:

To aid readers in navigating the intricate terminology of marketing automation and AI, the following glossary provides concise definitions of key terms used throughout this book:

Marketing Automation:

The use of technology and software to automate repetitive marketing tasks, streamline workflows, and optimize campaign management processes.

Artificial Intelligence (AI):

The development of computer systems capable of performing tasks that typically require human intelligence, such as learning, problem-solving, and decision-making.

Machine Learning (ML):

A subset of AI that involves the development of algorithms that allow computers to learn from data, recognize patterns, and make predictions or decisions without explicit programming.

Natural Language Processing (NLP):

A branch of AI that enables machines to understand, interpret, and generate human-like language.

Customer Segmentation:

The process of dividing a target audience into distinct groups based on shared characteristics, allowing for more targeted and personalized marketing strategies.

Lead Scoring:

The assignment of numerical values to leads based on their behavior, interactions, and characteristics, enabling prioritization and focus on leads more likely to convert.

Workflow Automation:

The use of technology to automate and streamline sequential steps and actions within a marketing campaign or business process.

Predictive Analytics:

The use of statistical algorithms and machine learning to analyze historical data and predict future trends or outcomes.

Chatbots:

AI-driven programs designed to simulate conversation with users, often used for customer support or interactive marketing.

Virtual Assistants:

AI-powered applications or devices that provide assistance to users through natural language processing and voice recognition.

Additional Resources for Further Reading:
Books

"Marketing Automation For Dummies" by Mathew Sweezey

"Artificial Intelligence: A Guide for Thinking Humans" by Melanie Mitchell

"HBR's 10 Must Reads on AI, Analytics, and the New Machine Age" by Harvard Business Review

Online Courses:

Coursera: "AI for Everyone" by Andrew Ng

LinkedIn Learning: "Marketing Automation Foundations" by Brad Batesole

edX: "Practical Deep Learning for Coders" by Jeremy Howard

Websites and Blogs:

HubSpot Academy (https://academy.hubspot.com/)

Neil Patel's Blog (https://neilpatel.com/blog/)

AI in Marketing (https://www.aiinmarketing.org/)

C. Index:

The index provides a comprehensive reference guide, allowing readers to quickly locate specific topics, terms, and concepts discussed throughout the book. Entries are organized alphabetically, providing a user-friendly tool for efficient navigation and reference.

This appendix aims to enhance the reader's experience by providing quick access to definitions, recommended resources for further exploration, and an index for easy reference. As you continue your exploration of marketing automation and AI, may these resources serve as valuable companions in your journey of discovery and implementation.

OTHER BOOKS BY THE AUTHOR

USINESS ETHICS AND CORPORATE SOCIALRESPONSIBILITY: CREATING A PURPOSE-DRIVEN COMPANY

SIDE HUSTLE HANDBOOK: EARNING EXTRA INCOME FOR FINANCIAL INDEPENDENCE

A GUIDE TO TRACKING CRYPTOCURRENCY WHALES: SCALE-UP YOUR CRYPTOCURRENCY PORTFOLIOS (10,000X)

Note Page 5..........................Date...............

Use this page for all writing during reading or study.

Note Page 5...........................Date................

Use this page for all writing during reading or study.

Use this page for all writing during reading or study.

Note Page 5...........................Date................

Use this page for all writing during reading or study.

Note Page 5...........................Date................

Use this page for all writing during reading or study.

Note Page 5.........................Date................

Use this page for all writing during reading or study.

Note Page 5...........................Date................

Use this page for all writing during reading or study.

Note Page 5..........................Date................

Use this page for all writing during reading or study.